4/13

D1562198

Sam Walton

Department Store Giant

Terri Dougherty

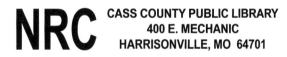

**BLACKBIRCH™
PRESS**

THOMSON

GALE

San Diego • Detroit • New York • San Francisco • Cleveland
New Haven, Conn. • Waterville, Maine • London • Munich

For more information, contact
The Gale Group, Inc.
27500 Drake Rd.
Farmington Hills, MI 48331-3535
Or you can visit our Internet site at http://www.gale.com

Photo Credits: cover, p. 34 © AP Photo/Danny Johnston; p. 5 © Diana Walker/Time Life Pictures/Getty Images; pp. 6–7 © Alan Schein Photography/CORBIS; p. 8 © Corbis; pp. 9, 13 © Bettmann/Corbis; p. 11 © Michael S. Lewis/Corbis; p. 14 © Oscar White/Corbis; pp. 16, 19, 21, 22, 24, 25, 27 29, 30, 35, 38, 43, 50, 51, 57 © Wal-Mart; p. 17 © Corel; p. 33 © Hulton Archive by Getty Images; p. 37 © John McGrail/Time Life Pictures/ Getty Images; pp. 39, 49 © Eli Reichman/Time Life Pictures/Getty Images; p. 41 © James Leynse/ Corbis Saba; p. 44 © Rob Nelson/Time Life Pictures/Getty Images; p. 45 © Steve Liss/Time Life Pictures/Getty Images; p. 46 © AP Photo/The Daily Sentinel, Andrew D. Brosig; pp. 47, 53 © Blackbirch Archives; p. 54 © Mark Peterson/Corbis Saba; p. 56 © Emile Wamsteker/ Bloomberg News/Landov; p. 58 © STR/AFP/Getty Images

LIBRARY OF CONGRESS CATALOGING-IN-PUBLICATION DATA

Dougherty, Terri.
  Sam Walton / by Terri Dougherty.
     p. cm. — (Giants of American industry)
  Summary: A brief biography of Wal-Mart founder Sam Walton, whose idea that he would get the best deals he could on merchandise and pass those savings on to the customer led to his becoming the richest man in America.
  Includes bibliographical references and index.
  ISBN 1-4103-0258-X (Hardback : alk. paper)
  1. Walton, Sam, 1918–1992—Juvenile literature. 2. Wal-Mart (Firm)—History—Juvenile literature. 3. Businesspeople—United States—Biography—Juvenile literature. 4. Billionaires—United States—Biography—Juvenile literature. [1. Walton, Sam, 1918–1992. 2. Businesspeople. 3. Wal-Mart (Firm)—History.] I. Title. II. Series.

  HC102.5.W35D68 2004
  381'.149'092—dc22   2003015180

Printed in China
10 9 8 7 6 5 4 3 2 1

CONTENTS

Wealth Not Important to America's Richest Man

In his lifetime, Sam Walton became the richest man in America; however, he bristled at the title. He had never cared about having more money than someone else. He did not build a huge retail empire in order to get rich. Making Wal-Mart grow was what made Walton happiest. The wealth the company brought him was not nearly as important as the enjoyment he got from running his business. Walton constantly put new ideas to work to make the company bigger and better, and the success of the business encouraged him to work even harder.

The Lure of Low Prices

Walton founded his Wal-Mart stores with the idea that he would get the best deals he could on merchandise. He would then pass those savings on to the customer. He might make a smaller profit on each deal, but the low prices would bring more people into his stores. Selling more goods to more people would make his business a resounding success.

Walton remained dedicated to this idea all his life. He did not waver from his belief that Wal-Mart should spend as little money as possible in order to keep prices low. For example, the company needed airplanes so Walton and others could travel to stores quickly. Instead of buying fancy new planes, Walton bought used ones at economical prices. Throughout his life, Walton kept a practical view of how money should be spent. He had grown up during the Great Depression when money was scarce, so he knew what it was like to have very little. His frugal ways helped the company expand and stay successful.

When he opened his first Wal-Mart in July 1962, Sam Walton never dreamed that in less than twenty-five years he would become the richest man in America.

As Wal-Mart's success grew, Walton occasionally took time out to hunt and to play tennis. His real love, though, was his work with Wal-Mart. He was dedicated to his job and truly enjoyed it. Even when he took vacations with his wife and family to places around the world, he thought about business. Wherever he went, Walton poked his head into stores to see how other companies did things and to find ideas he could use in his own business.

A Down-to-Earth Personality

Wealth and success did not make Walton aloof, however. He had a humble, folksy personality that made people feel at ease. He was a good listener and created enthusiasm for Wal-Mart among his employees. Whether he was leading a company cheer or sharing ideas with his employees, whom he called associates, he remained approachable.

Walton did not pamper himself with luxuries. He was not a miser, however. He bought what he needed and lived comfortably in a nice home and with enough land for hunting. He traveled with his wife and children and stayed at expensive resorts. He did not, however, show off his wealth or pass his time thinking of things he could buy. He spent it doing what he truly enjoyed—he worked at Wal-Mart.

In 2003, Fortune *magazine named Wal-Mart the most admired company in America.*

Tough Years on the Farm

Samuel Moore Walton was born on March 29, 1918, to Thomas Walton and Nannia Lee Lawrence Walton. The Waltons lived on a farm near Kingfisher, Oklahoma. Samuel's brother, Bud, was born three years later.

Thomas Walton's farm did well for a while, but the family struggled when crop prices fell. At one point, Thomas traded the family's farm for another near Omega, Oklahoma. After a few tough years, Thomas gave up farming. He went to work for his

Unlike other families (pictured) who were forced to move from town to town in search of work during the Great Depression, Sam's family moved because his father's job required it.

8

uncle's farm mortgage business, where his job was to evict farmers from their land when they could not repay their loans. The Waltons moved to various towns in Oklahoma and Missouri so Thomas could work. He was fortunate to have a job. Employment was hard to come by during the Great Depression of the 1930s.

The Waltons were living in Springfield, Missouri, when Sam started school. He had always been a curious child. When he was three, he had wandered away from home and ambled into a school building, where he listened quietly to the teacher until his mother finally found him.

Eagle Scout

Friendly and upbeat, Sam was able to make friends quickly whenever his family moved to a new town. For a time, the Waltons lived in Marshall, Missouri, and then Shelbina, Missouri, where Sam started high school. When the family lived in Marshall, he made a bet with some other boys that he would become the first of them to earn the rank of Eagle Scout. He won the bet after the family moved to Shelbina. He saved a boy from drowning, and at the age of thirteen became the youngest Eagle Scout in Missouri at that time.

During the Depression, Sam often traveled with his father, whose job was evicting farmers (pictured) from their land when they could not repay their loans.

When he was not in school, Sam sometimes went along with his father as he repossessed farms. He saw firsthand the poverty people lived in, and the tragic situations of the farmers made an impact on the young man. He never liked to waste money, and his parents reinforced this value by being very careful about how they spent the little money they had.

Sam also saw how his father conducted business. His job was hard on Sam's dad, but he was honest and tried to leave the farmers with some self-respect. Sam also noticed his father did not make a large amount of money on one deal. Instead, he made a small profit on many deals.

9

Work and Study

Sam was already working by the time he was seven or eight years old. He sold magazine subscriptions and also raised and sold rabbits and pigeons. In seventh grade, he started a newspaper route. "I learned from a very early age that it was important for us kids to help provide for the home, to be contributors rather than just takers," he said. "In the process, of course, we learned how much hard work it took to get your hands on a dollar, and that when you did it was worth something."[1]

Because his mother wanted Sam and his brother to go to college, the family moved to Columbia, Missouri, in 1933. Sam's mother had dropped out of college after she married and thought that living in Columbia, home to the University of Missouri, would give her sons a good chance of continuing their education. In Columbia, they would meet university students who could motivate them to attend college. The Waltons rented the upstairs rooms of their brick house to students, and Sam also met students through his paper route. Sam's mother encouraged her sons to study hard and always do their best.

School Leader

Sam was very competitive. When he was a freshman in high school in Shelbina, he went out for the football team even though he weighed only about 130 pounds. He continued to play football in high school in Columbia, as quarterback on offense and as linebacker on defense. He could motivate people and saw the value of teamwork as his team went undefeated and won the state championship. He also played basketball, although at five-foot-nine he thought at first that he was too short to go out for the team. He kept hanging around the gym, though, and was asked to play as a guard when he was a senior. His leadership helped the team become undefeated state champions.

Sam extended his love of leadership to school clubs and became vice president of his junior class and student council president. He was voted most versatile boy in high school. Asked to address the senior class at graduation, he titled his speech "Leadership." Even with all his other activities, he still found time to work. He delivered newspapers and sold milk from the family cow after football practice.

10

As a student at the University of Missouri (pictured), Sam became known as "Hustler Walton" because he joined so many organizations.

There were several reasons for his busy schedule. He was very motivated and focused on success, but he also wanted to keep his mind off the tension in the Walton home. His dad traveled often, the family had financial difficulties, and his parents did not get along. Sam stayed busy in order to get away from the discord at home. He vowed that his own family would never see the kind of arguing his parents engaged in, and he continued to keep his schedule full of activities as he entered the University of Missouri in 1936.

"Hustler Walton"

Walton wanted to meet as many people as he could at the University of Missouri. He knew this would help him win leadership positions in the many organizations he joined. He greeted other students with a cheery "hello" on his way to class. He made a point to speak to them first and to call as many people as he could by name. "Before long, I probably knew more students than anybody in the university, and they recognized me and considered me their friend,"[2] he said.

Walton joined so many organizations that a campus newspaper article referred to him as "Hustler Walton." He loved to run for

11

office. He became president of the senior men's honor society, his senior class, and a Bible class made up of college students. He joined a fraternity and became an officer in it. He also joined the ROTC, the Reserve Officer Training Corps, which prepared men for military leadership. Walton was chosen as president of an ROTC club.

A Hardworking Student

Walton also met people through the jobs he held while going to college. He had to work so he could earn money to pay for his clothes, food, tuition, and books. His parents did not have any extra money to pay for those things. Walton had been self-sufficient since he graduated from high school.

While in college he turned his paper route into a business. He added more routes and hired helpers to deliver some papers for him. He made thousands of dollars with his paper route business—enough money to buy a car as well as pay for the other things he needed. In addition to his newspaper route, Walton also worked in a restaurant and was the head lifeguard at a swimming pool.

Walton majored in economics and considered careers in law, politics, and insurance. After he graduated in 1940, he thought about going to the Wharton School of Finance in Pennsylvania but decided it was too expensive.

He also thought about working in a retail store. A family neighbor who owned a variety store talked to Sam about retailing. Sam admired the man and how he had gone from being a barber to starting, with his brothers, a variety store chain that grew to sixty stores. Before he graduated, Sam had job interviews with Sears, Roebuck and Company and J.C. Penney Company, Inc. He received job offers from both companies and chose J.C. Penney. Three days after he graduated from college, Walton left Columbia, Missouri, for Des Moines, Iowa. He began work as a management trainee at the J.C. Penney store, where he earned seventy-five dollars a month.

No Future in Retail?

Walton fell in love with retailing. He enjoyed selling, and his job at the J.C. Penney store convinced him his future was in retail. He almost loved selling too much, however. Part of his job was to

Right after his college graduation, Walton began work as a management trainee at a J.C. Penney store (pictured) in Des Moines, Iowa.

keep track of how much merchandise he sold and how much money the store made. He was usually so eager to meet with customers that he did not pay enough attention to paperwork. One company official thought he was not cut out for retail because his sales slips were so mixed up.

Walton, though, made up for his sloppy record keeping with hard work. He worked from 6:30 A.M. to 7 or 8 P.M., and during his lunch hour he would visit other stores to see what he could learn from them. On Sunday, he would go to his manager's house

James Cash Penney (pictured) visited his Des Moines store when Walton was an employee there. Walton was impressed with Penney's attention to details affecting both customers and store costs.

to play cards and talk about the retail business with other men who worked for the company. One of the highlights of his days with J.C. Penney was when the store's founder, James Cash Penney, visited the Des Moines store. Walton remembered years later that Penney showed him how to nicely tie a package with as little paper and twine as possible. Penney's attention to detail made an impression on Walton. His package-tying example showed Walton that a customer needed to be treated well, but that the employee should also keep the store's cost in mind. The Penney visit also made Walton notice how much of an impression it can make on employees when the company founder walks into a store.

Army Service

After a year and half, Walton left his job. The United States had entered World War II in 1941, and he expected he would soon be called up for military service. He volunteered for the armed forces but was found to have a heart irregularity. He moved to Oklahoma in January 1942 while he waited for a noncombat assignment.

While he waited to be called up by the army, Walton worked at a gunpowder factory near Tulsa, Oklahoma. He lived in Claremore, twenty miles from his job. It was there that he met his future wife, Helen Robson, when she was twenty-two.

Marriage and Family

Helen was with a date at a bowling alley when Walton first saw her. She finished her turn, returned to her seat, and saw Walton in one of wooden chairs. He broke the ice by asking, "Haven't I met you somewhere before?"[3] He later called her and asked her for a date. They began to see each other, and after they had dated for a few months, he was called up for military service. They decided to get married, and he came home on a three-day leave for the ceremony on February 14, 1943.

The couple went west, where Walton served as director of security at a POW camp and also at aircraft plants in California and Utah. He planned to return to retailing after his time with the army ended and kept up with the business while he was in the military. He read books on retailing and visited department stores to study how they were run. By the time the war was over in 1945, he was ready to start his own business.

By this time, he had a family to support. The Waltons' first son, Samuel Robson Walton, was born on October 28, 1944. Rob, as he was nicknamed, was followed by three more children. John Thomas was born in 1946, James Carr in 1948, and Alice in 1949.

Store Owner

The Waltons had to decide which town would be their home. Walton considered going into the department store business with a friend in St. Louis, Missouri. Helen hesitated, however. She did not want to live in a big city and did not like the idea of Walton going into business with a partner. She was afraid their partnership could turn sour.

Walton borrowed money from his father-in-law to open his first store, the franchised Ben Franklin store pictured here, in Newport, Arkansas.

The couple decided to set up shop in the small town of Newport, Arkansas. To finance the venture, Walton borrowed twenty thousand dollars from Helen's father. He also used five thousand dollars of his and his wife's savings to buy a Ben Franklin variety store. He rented the store building and owned the franchise. As a franchise owner, Walton bought most of the store's merchandise through Butler Brothers, which franchised Ben Franklin stores. He also paid a fee for the right to use the Ben Franklin name on his store. In return, Butler Brothers helped Walton learn how to run his business. The company told him what items to sell and how much to charge for them. Like other Ben Franklin stores, Walton's sold cleaning supplies, makeup, and clothing.

Driven by Deals

Walton also had his own ideas, however. Although he bought some of the goods for his store through Butler Brothers, he also bought some directly from product manufacturers. This allowed him to charge a lower price on these items than other stores in town could. Walton wanted to buy goods at the lowest price possible so he could pass the savings on to customers and attract more people to his store. He would make a smaller profit on each sale, but would sell more goods. He was tireless in his pursuit of deals. He would learn about a good price on a product and at night would drive to places like Union City, Tennessee, to pick up goods such as shirts and underwear, so the merchandise could be in the store first thing in the morning.

Walton was driven to beat the competition. He continued to read about retailing and to study other stores. There was another variety store across the street from his Ben Franklin store, and he would often walk over to check out the displays and prices. When he heard that the store was going to expand into the building next to it, Walton quickly drove to Hot Springs and persuaded the building owner to lease the space to him instead of his competitor. He put his own department store into the building rather than let another store owner have more space.

Walton's Ben Franklin was the first business in Newport to sell soft-serve ice cream.

Walton did everything he could think of to attract customers. One day he put his popcorn machine outside so customers would smell it for blocks. He also bought the first soft-serve ice cream machine in the town. He thought he was taking quite a chance by borrowing eighteen hundred dollars from the bank for the machine, but his idea worked. Customers came into the store to buy ice cream made by the machine.

Painful Lesson

After three years, Walton had earned enough money to repay the loan he had received from his father-in-law. He became involved in the Newport community and was president of the chamber of commerce. He also found time for hunting and fishing. He spent some time with his growing family, but often worked late into the night. Walton's hard work had made the store a success. It had been losing money before Walton bought it, but by 1950, it was the top Ben Franklin store in a six-state region.

Walton was not the only person who was aware of the store's success. His landlord also noticed how well the store was doing. When Walton bought the business, he had agreed to rent the store for five years. When the lease was up, his landlord decided not to renew it. He wanted his son to run the successful store instead. There was nowhere else in town for Walton to move the business, so he had to sell it to the landlord.

The family hated to leave Newport, but they had no choice. Walton would have to look for a new town where he could run a business. It was a painful lesson for Walton. He learned he needed to go through the details of his business deals thoroughly, down to the length of the lease.

Bentonville

Walton's father-in-law helped him find another store to run. Walton had made fifty thousand dollars when he sold the store in Newport and wanted to invest it in another business. He and his father-in-law looked at stores in towns in northwest Arkansas. Helen wanted to live in that area because it was close to her family in Claremore, Oklahoma. Sam liked the region because it was close to the borders of Kansas and Missouri. Living there would let him take advantage of quail-hunting seasons in those states as well as in Oklahoma and Arkansas.

The Waltons found a store for sale in Bentonville. With a population of three thousand, the town was smaller than Newport, which had seven thousand people. Walton, however, felt he could make the store successful.

Walton remodeled the store and expanded it into space next door. When it opened on July 29, 1950, it offered free balloons for children and clothespins for nine cents. The store was a Ben Franklin franchise, as Walton's store in Newport had been. His new store, however, was called Walton's Five and Dime. As he had done in Newport, Walton bought most of his goods from Butler Brothers and used the Ben Franklin system for setting prices. He continued to search for deals and one time drove to New York City to buy thong sandals that he sold for nineteen cents a pair.

In 1950, Walton opened this Walton's Five and Dime, one of the first self-service stores in the country, in Bentonville, Arkansas.

Self-Service

Walton decided to put a new idea into practice at the Bentonville store. At that time, shoppers got items from clerks who were stationed at cash registers around a store. The clerks got goods off the shelves for the customer. Walton heard about stores where customers served themselves. Customers walked around the store with a basket and selected what they wanted to buy. They paid for their purchases at the front of the store.

Walton liked this self-service idea because it would let him employ fewer people. This would lower his costs, and he could charge less for his merchandise. This would bring even more customers into his stores. Walton stuck to the strategy that had worked so well in Newport: He would charge as low a price as he could for items. Although he would make a smaller profit on each item, he would sell more, which put him ahead in the end.

A Family Enterprise

The store was successful, and Walton jumped into community activities in Bentonville, as he had in Newport. With his children in mind, he also helped start a Little League baseball program and helped sponsor the high school football team.

His four children were part of Walton's retail business as well. They helped by carrying boxes of goods to the upstairs of the store. His father-in-law, Leland Stanford Robson, encouraged Walton to set up his business as a family partnership. Walton admired Robson's business sense and followed his advice in 1953 when he set up Walton Enterprises, a partnership with his wife and children. All of the profits from the store went into the partnership. The children also invested money they earned from their newspaper routes into the business.

The amount of time Walton dedicated to his business meant that Walton was often away from his family. When he was home for dinner he often sat down and read. It was difficult at times for Helen to manage at home with four children. The family also, however, took long vacations together in the summer, camping and traveling to national parks. The family enjoyed the time they spent together and became very close.

Another Store

Walton's store in Bentonville was so successful that he decided to open another in Fayetteville, twenty miles away. The new store was also called Walton's Five and Dime, but it was not a Ben Franklin franchise. This allowed Walton to buy merchandise from anyone he chose, but also meant that he did not have the support of a big company behind him to advertise and buy goods. To get merchandise for the store, the manager would have to order from salespeople. Walton would also make trips to Tennessee, load goods into his station wagon, and bring them to the store in Fayetteville.

Walton continued to spend as little as he could to run his business. He kept his stores clean and looking nice by displaying merchandise on metal shelves, but refused to waste money on things like a big office for himself. His first office in the Bentonville store was a small one in the back that he could enter only by climbing a ladder. He later moved his office to an old garage that he remodeled.

Walton's Five and Dime in Fayetteville, Arkansas, was not a franchise because Walton wanted to be able to buy merchandise from anyone he chose.

A New Idea

Walton's success with his stores in Bentonville and Fayetteville made him decide to open another store. He learned that a shopping center was being built in Ruskin Heights, near Kansas City, Missouri. A shopping center was a new idea at that time. The center would have a grocery store, drugstore, small shops, and a Ben Franklin store. Walton wanted to run the Ben Franklin store but did not have enough money to buy the franchise on his own. He asked his brother, Bud, to invest some money in the store with him. Bud had been trained in store management at a J.C. Penney store, just as Sam had. He had worked for Sam for a time, and was then managing his own store in Versailles, Missouri. He agreed to

21

the idea, and the brothers made the investment. The store did better than Walton dreamed. "If I ever had any doubts about the potential of the business we were in, Ruskin Heights ended them," he said. "That thing took off like a house afire."[4]

Even so, it was the shopping center idea rather than more stores that interested Walton at first. He decided he would become a developer and open shopping centers in Arkansas. He did not have enough money to do it on his own, however, and the idea was so new that he had a hard time finding other people to invest money in the project. He spent two years and twenty-five thousand dollars in an attempt to build a shopping mall in Little Rock before he decided to give up.

"Success Story of the Year"

Afterward, Walton was ready to concentrate all of his energy on opening more retail stores. In the mid-1950s, he learned to fly and bought his first airplane so he could visit his stores more quickly. The airplane also let him fly over cities to scout out locations for new stores. He loved the fact that he did not have to

Walton bought an airplane and learned how to fly it so he could scout out locations for new stores and visit his existing stores more easily.

worry about driving over winding roads to visit his stores—he could just fly to them in a straight line. He could also make use of his time by putting the airplane on autopilot and doing paperwork while he flew.

He soon had more stores to visit. Along with Bud and some other partners, he opened three variety stores in Arkansas and two in Kansas. When he made money in one store, he would invest it by buying a new one. By 1960, he owned fifteen stores and was doing $1.4 million a year in business. A local magazine called him the "success story of the year."

Family Centers and Discount Stores

Walton did not think he was successful enough, however. He began to build larger stores that he called family centers. Because they were bigger than variety stores, they could do more business. This brought in more money and profits for Walton's company.

Discounting was another idea that interested Walton. Discount stores first appeared in the 1930s, and by the 1960s were making their mark on the American retail scene. Discounters focused on price and sold every product as cheaply as they could. The stores were plain, in order to keep costs down. Walton knew his variety stores could not compete with discount stores. He could sell a few items for very low prices, but not as many as discount stores could.

Walton knew small-town retailing and felt that discount stores would do well in the small towns like the ones in which his variety stores were located. He knew people did not want to drive three or four hours to larger cities to get bargain prices. He wanted to give them those bargains in their hometowns.

Wal-Mart Is Born

Walton was not sure he was ready to go into the venture alone, however. He knew he would need a good system to get merchandise into the stores. He asked Butler Brothers to supply the merchandise for his new discount store, but company officials refused. They did not like the discount store idea, and did not think it would work.

Undaunted, Walton decided to do it himself. He and his wife borrowed most of the money they needed to open the first Wal-Mart in Rogers, Arkansas, near Bentonville. Bud and the store

In the 1960s, discount stores began to have an impact on retail in American cities. Walton decided to introduce such stores to small-town America.

manager invested a small amount, but most of the money came from the Waltons. The first Wal-Mart opened on July 2, 1962. Its sign announced Walton's philosophy: "We Sell for Less" and "Satisfaction Guaranteed."

The new Wal-Mart store upset the officials at Butler Brothers. There was already a Ben Franklin store in Rogers, owned by someone other than Walton, and Butler Brothers did not want Walton's discount store competing with the Ben Franklin variety store. They told him not to open any more Wal-Marts. Walton did not listen, however. He wanted to open discount stores in small towns before anyone else did. He opened his second and third Wal-Marts, in Harrison and Springdale, Arkansas, in 1964.

Unsightly Beginning

The first Wal-Mart stores were not pretty. In one store, clothing racks were hung from metal pipes. Other items were stacked on tables. There was no air-conditioning. Walton spent as little on the stores as he could. One of the first Wal-Marts was located in a building that had formerly housed a Coca-Cola bottling plant.

Walton was not worried about how the stores looked because he was intent on bringing customers into his store with low

On July 2, 1962, crowds gathered for the grand opening of the first Wal-Mart store in Rogers, Arkansas.

prices. He made a big production out of every store that opened, offering deals and special events. At one grand opening, he provided watermelon and donkey rides. The weather was extremely hot, however, and the watermelons burst. The juice ran all over the parking lot and mixed with the dung from the donkeys. Customers tracked the mixture through the store. It was a mess.

Customers forgave Walton, though, because they loved Wal-Mart's low prices. They drove for miles to get bargains such as toothpaste for twenty-seven cents a tube. Walton was able to offer such prices because when he got a good deal from a supplier, he always passed the low price on to his customers.

Success and Long Days

Walton kept his variety store businesses, but focused most of the company's resources on opening new Wal-Mart stores. By 1969, Walton had opened eighteen Wal-Marts and had fourteen variety stores. The Wal-Marts were built in small towns with populations of five thousand to twenty-five thousand, where people did not have access to discount stores as they did in large cities. The lack of competition proved to be valuable for Wal-Mart, and the stores did well. One of the stores Walton opened was in Newport, Arkansas, where he had lost his lease on his first store years before. The store he had once managed closed because of competition from Wal-Mart.

The expanding business kept Walton busier than ever. He no longer had time for leadership positions in clubs or a spot on the city council. He wanted to keep a close eye on the people who managed his stores, and he spent much of his time flying from one store to another. His managers had to fill out reports each week and month so he could make sure they were doing things the way he wanted.

Walton often began his day at 4 or 5 A.M. with breakfast at a downtown coffee shop. He drove an old pickup truck to work, and if he decided to visit stores that day, he would fly off in his airplane to do so. When he returned, around 6 P.M., he expected other company managers to meet with him to talk over what he had learned on his trip.

Walton sometimes took a few hours off in the afternoon to go quail hunting or play tennis. He took vacations with his family, such as camping trips in the Ozark Mountains. Even on vacation,

Walton built a large warehouse and company headquarters (pictured) in Bentonville, Arkansas, as the center of his new system for the efficient delivery of goods.

though, he could not let go of his love of retailing. While his wife and children enjoyed the campground or resort, he went into town to check out competitors' stores.

New Headquarters

Walton thought of little besides making Wal-Mart grow. He had thirty-two stores in 1970. He wanted to make them run more efficiently, and so he began to use computers to keep track of his records.

He also needed a better way to get goods to his stores. Trucking companies and other distributors of merchandise did not make regular stops at stores in small country towns. Walton's managers had to pay the trucking companies to make a special trip when they needed goods. This was inefficient, so Walton and his employees put together a centralized system for getting goods to stores. A large headquarters and warehouse were built in Bentonville. Trucking companies brought the merchandise to Bentonville, and from there, Wal-Mart trucks took it to Walton's stores.

Stock Sale

Walton's discount stores were doing well, and he believed he could do even better if he built more stores. He had already borrowed heavily, however, to build stores, the headquarters, and the distribution center. He had borrowed so much that it was becoming difficult for him to persuade banks to lend him more money. He had had to go to New York to try to persuade larger lending institutions to lend him money. They were not as familiar with Wal-Mart as his local banks were, and they were not certain that he could pay back his loans.

Walton disliked asking lenders for money. He also did not like being in debt. If the company could not pay back its loans, he would be in trouble. He decided that to bring more money into the company, he would have to sell stock.

In the past, Walton had always borrowed money from lenders to expand his company, then used store profits to pay back the loans. Selling stock, by contrast, would be like borrowing from investors. People would pay money to buy stock in the company, and Walton would use the money to build more stores. The stock would be worth more money as the company grew and increased its profits because other people would be willing to pay a higher price for the stock, and its value would increase.

Walton was excited about the prospect of using cash from a stock sale to build more stores, but he was also concerned. Selling stock to people outside the family would give these investors a say in how the business was run. He did not want to lose control of the company or risk having it taken over by someone outside the family.

He solved this problem by keeping most of the stock in the hands of Walton Enterprises, Inc., the partnership made up of Walton, his wife, and their children. Walton knew he and his family would never sell their stock. Twenty-three percent of the company's stock, three hundred thousand shares, were offered for sale to the public on October 1, 1970. The sale brought in more than $4 million for the company.

The stock sale was a huge relief to Walton. He no longer had to worry about being deeply in debt and personally responsible for paying off the company's loans. He would not need to ask lenders for more money. He was satisfied that, as majority shareholder in Wal-Mart, he would continue to control the company.

In October 1970, Walton (pictured here, center, at the New York Stock Exchange) offered three hundred thousand shares of company stock to the public. The $4 million sale enabled Wal-Mart to expand further.

Deeply Involved

The stock sale gave Walton the money he needed to open more stores. He could take Wal-Mart farther away from its Bentonville roots. By January 1973, there were fifty-five Wal-Marts in Arkansas, Missouri, Kansas, Oklahoma, and Louisiana. He also owned nine variety stores.

Walton wanted to keep Wal-Mart's growth orderly. He would open a store within a day's drive of the distribution center in Bentonville and then open stores in the towns around it until the area was filled with Wal-Marts. He would then move into another region. All of the stores were in small towns or well outside the center of a larger city.

The 1970 sale of stock was so successful that, by 1974, the Wal-Mart chain had expanded to seventy-eight stores in eight states, including this store in Salem, Missouri.

As Wal-Mart grew, Walton continued to stay involved with every aspect of the organization. He decided where to build stores, how they would be built, and what products they would carry. He also visited stores frequently so he could motivate managers and employees. "I stick my fingers into everything I can to see how it's coming along,"[5] he said. He also spied on the competition—he went into Kmart and Sears stores and asked questions of their managers.

He had a great memory for numbers and had an excellent way of motivating people. He had a folksy charm and made it a point to talk to employees of every level. He gained their respect by asking them their opinions and getting them to tell him what was on their minds. He made all employees feel as though they made a difference in how the company was run and how profitable it was.

He made it a point to call his employees "associates." The word had been used by his first employer, J.C. Penney, to describe his employees, and Walton was reminded of the term while on a trip to England. He passed by a sign on a business that listed all of the "associates" who worked there. Walton brought the term back to Wal-Mart as a way to address his employees in a respectful manner.

Walton's weakness, though, was organization. He did not slow down long enough to worry about details, such as where his briefcase was. He left it to his secretary to track it down at an airport or another company. He would often leave the office on the spur of the moment to visit stores without checking first to see if business associates were scheduled to meet with him that day. His mind was always working too fast to stick to a schedule.

Retirement?

By 1974 Wal-Mart was a powerful regional discount chain with seventy-eight stores in eight states. The stock price had risen, and family members and employees who had bought the company's stock at a low price saw their investment grow. Walton's business was more successful than he could have ever dreamed it would be.

His wife urged him to start cutting back on his schedule. By 1974 the fifty-six-year-old Walton had run his own business for twenty-nine years. His children had graduated from college, and the couple wanted to travel abroad. Walton decided to step back and let others run the day-to-day operations of Wal-Mart. He appointed Ronald M. Mayer as chairman and chief executive officer of the company, and he took the title of chairman of the board's executive committee.

Walton still owned the majority of stock in the company, though, and was still interested in how the business was being run. He tried to enjoy his less hectic life but was unable to forget about Wal-Mart. True to old habits, he visited stores while he traveled, to seek out new ideas for Wal-Mart. On a trip to a tennis ball factory in South Korea, he saw employees do a company cheer and brought that idea back to Wal-Mart. Although he was supposed to simply offer advice to the new chief executive officer, that advice became orders that had to be followed.

Back in Charge

Without Walton as the company's day-to-day leader, however, things did not go smoothly at Wal-Mart. There were rifts between executives who vied for power. Employees who backed one executive or the other stopped exchanging information that was vital to the company's growth. Walton could not bear to see employees take sides and plug the lines of communication he had worked so hard to establish. His life had been Wal-Mart, and he realized he could not step back. In 1976, Mayer left the company, and Walton resumed his role as chairman and chief executive.

He did not have an easy job ahead of him, however. Many executives who backed Mayer left the company when he did. Others left because they felt Walton had overlooked them for promotions. Walton rallied his employees and encouraged them to work as a team. He hired David Glass, who had been working at a discount drug chain in Illinois, as an executive vice president. He felt he had the talented employees he needed to face the competition Wal-Mart was receiving from other stores.

New Challenges

Wal-Mart was facing new challenges. Kmart had opened stores in some of the small towns where Wal-Mart stores were located and was trying to take away Wal-Mart's customers. In order to keep its customers, Wal-Mart would have to keep an eye on Kmart's prices and price its products the same as its competitor. At one point, both the Wal-Mart and Kmart stores in Little Rock priced toothpaste at six cents a tube. Wal-Mart's strategy of meeting Kmart's prices worked, and it retained its customers.

In the late 1970s, Kmart opened stores in the same small towns where Wal-Marts were located. By matching such competitors' prices, Wal-Mart was able to keep its customers.

By 1979, Wal-Mart was selling a billion dollars of merchandise each year. The variety stores had been phased out, and the discount stores were booming. Walton had expected to eventually reach the billion-dollar sales mark, but the company did it a year earlier than even he predicted. "Of all the milestones we ever reached, that one probably impressed me the most," Walton said. "I have to admit, I was amazed that Wal-Mart had turned into a billion-dollar company."[6]

Risky Business

Wal-Mart had reached a goal Walton had set for the company years earlier, but Walton wanted it to continue to grow. In 1980, there were 276 Wal-Mart stores in eleven states, but the company was still small compared to Kmart and Sears.

Wal-Mart usually expanded by building new stores, but when Walton heard that another discount chain was for sale, he thought it might be time for the company to grow through acquisition. The purchase of Kuhn's Big K, a chain of more than one hundred stores, would quickly raise the number of Wal-Mart stores.

Sam Walton remained actively involved in the day-to-day operations of his stores by frequently visiting his stores and talking with employees at all levels.

It was a risky move, however. Not all of the stores in the other chain were profitable. Walton would have to take the good with the bad and gamble that the good stores would turn a profit in the end. He mulled over the decision for two years.

Walton discussed the idea with the company's executive committee. Committee members showed their opinions with a vote. Half of the executives thought the company should go ahead and buy the stores, while half thought the move was too risky. The responsibility of making the final decision rested on Walton.

Walton had a gut feeling that the move would work. He decided to buy the stores, and in 1981, Wal-Mart brought the chain into its fold. It closed some of the stores that were not doing well and converted the rest to Wal-Marts. It was not easy to blend the new stores into the Wal-Mart way of doing things, and there were some problems with distributing goods to the new stores because many were farther away from the Bentonville distribution center than other Wal-Mart stores. In the end, however, it was a success. The stores became a profitable addition to the Wal-Mart chain. The expansion put the company into position for even more growth.

Walton was more confident than he had ever been. From then on it was common for the company to open 100 to 150 new stores a year. There was no limit to what he thought the company could do.

Saturday Morning Meetings

The company had grown to 491 stores by 1982, and Walton was still its lifeblood. He wrote messages to employees in the company's *Wal-Mart World* publication, in which he shared things such as his sorrow at the death of his hunting dog, Ol' Roy. He would interact with employees of all levels when he visited a store, look people in the eye, ask questions, and listen to their ideas.

Walton loved to motivate employees. One of the important ways the company did this was to hold Saturday morning meetings. Associates had to work on Saturdays, so Walton felt management people should, too. He would bring high- and low-level employees together for meetings that became events. He would go

Walton scheduled store meetings on Saturday mornings because he believed that since associates had to work on Saturdays, those in management should, too.

to work at 3 A.M. so he could go over sales figures from each store, see which ones were performing well, and bring up compliments or concerns at the meeting. Financial reports were only a small part of the meetings, though, and associates never knew quite what to expect. Walton would spice things up with an employee singing group or seed-spitting contest. The 7:30 A.M. meetings would begin with Walton doing the University of Arkansas Razorback cheer, which resembled a farmer calling a pig with the words "Woooo Pig Soooooey!" He also led the Wal-Mart cheer, yelling out each letter and wiggling for the dash. The cheer ended with "Who's number one? The customer!!"[7]

Not Too Cool to Hula

Walton wanted his employees, who often called him Mr. Sam, to be as dedicated to serving customers as he was. He expected managers and executives to work long hours. He was a boss who felt that his employees should work hard, and he was able to motivate them with his enthusiasm and informal style.

Although the company had reached $4 billion in sales by 1983, Walton wanted to continue to treat it like a small business that had a sense of community among its employees. Employees were invited to annual meetings held in his large backyard. The meetings were meant to impress investors and stock analysts, as well as foster employee morale. Walton would give out awards and might sing the "Star-Spangled Banner." Guests included politicians such as Bill Clinton, who was then governor of Arkansas.

Walton also proved that no one in the company was in too high a position to do something silly in order to delight and inspire fellow employees. Although he was somewhat embarrassed, he did a hula dance on Wall Street in 1984 when the company reached a high sales goal. "We break down barriers, which helps us communicate better with one another," Walton said. "And we make our people feel part of a family in which no one is too important or too puffed up to lead a cheer or be the butt of a joke."[8]

Appreciation from Bentonville

Walton had a knack for making people feel as if they knew him, which was evident when the town of Bentonville honored him and Helen in 1983 with Sam and Helen Walton Appreciation Day. As people passed by in a parade, he called many by name. Tears

When his company reached a high sales goal, Walton did a hula dance on Wall Street to show that no one was too important to do something silly to inspire fellow employees.

formed in his eyes as he thanked the town. Although the town was honoring him and his wife for supporting the community and keeping the company's headquarters there, he said the community had in reality supported him for thirty years. "We owed the most money at the banks, and [our children] had the most broken bones. With four lively children who climbed trees and played football, we had a lot of fractures," he said. "But we always managed to get the youngsters patched up and our loans paid. We could not have done it without your patronage and support."[9]

Walton felt that keeping the company headquarters in Bentonville gave him an advantage in the retail world. He liked being in the out-of-the-way community, away from his competitors who often underestimated what a force in retail he truly was. He was known nationwide for his company's success, however. One of the people who complimented him on the appreciation day was President Ronald Reagan. Bill Clinton also congratulated him, as did Vice President George Bush.

In 1983, Bentonville declared a Sam and Helen Walton Appreciation Day to honor the Waltons for their support of the community and for keeping the company headquarters there.

Walton opened Hypermarts, which carried both groceries and general merchandise, in the 1980s. The Hypermarts were not as successful as most of Walton's other business ideas.

Taking Chances

No matter how big and successful Wal-Mart grew, Walton never stopped looking for new ideas in order to get the best out of his employees and his company. In 1980, he visited a store in Crowley, Louisiana, that had a greeter at the front door. The person both welcomed customers and watched for shoplifters. Walton liked the idea so much that he pushed for all his stores to have greeters.

Many of the ideas that Walton tried, such as the greeters, self-service, and mass discounting, were successful. Not all of his ideas worked, however. A chain of discount drug and home improvement stores did not make enough money. Walton decided to open Hypermarts, giant stores that sold both groceries and general merchandise. These types of stores were successful in other parts of the world. Several Hypermarts were opened and were marginally profitable, but the stores did not make enough money for Walton to consider them a success.

Walton decided that opening the giant stores had been a mistake, but he did not worry about it. Just as he recovered from the bad lease deal in Newport, he rebounded and moved on. He decided the Hypermarts were too big, so he opened smaller stores called Supercenters that, like Hypermarts, carried both groceries and general merchandise. This smaller version of the concept worked.

Walton even took chances when his life depended on it. In 1982, he was diagnosed with leukemia. Traditional treatment involved surgery and chemotherapy, but there was also an experimental drug called interferon that had been showing promising results. Walton did not like the idea of surgery, and he spent a month gathering information and thinking over his decision. He agreed to try the new drug, which involved giving himself injections. The treatment worked, and the disease went into remission.

While Walton enjoyed entertaining new ideas, he was never fond of spending money. When it came to technology, other Wal-Mart executives often had to talk him into moving forward. He reluctantly agreed to spend millions on a satellite system in 1983 that would help speed product information to stores and would also allow him to reach employees on the company's own satellite television station.

Sam's Club

Walton was also interested in selling to customers through wholesale clubs. These clubs sold goods that moved quickly, everything from mustard to furniture. The buildings were not fancy. They resembled warehouses—the goods were stocked on wooden pallets, and customers walked on concrete floors. The stores offered a relatively small selection of products, but at prices that were extremely low. Customers had to pay a fee to shop in the stores and usually bought items in large quantities.

Walton began to explore the idea in the early 1980s. He visited Price Club stores in California and took note of how the merchandise was displayed and how the stores were built. He had always taken ideas from competitors, but at a Price Club in San Diego, California, he got caught when he was gathering information on prices and store display ideas. An employee found him making notes about prices on a tape recorder. The store had a policy against people using tape recorders in its store, and the employee told him the tape would have to be erased. Walton knew that he was in the wrong because his stores had the same

*Inspired by a Price Club store he visited in California,
Walton opened the first Sam's Wholesale Club in Oklahoma
City in 1983.*

policy about tape recorders. He knew the store owner, however, and got the tape back after writing a nice note to him.

The incident did not prevent Walton from opening his warehouse stores. The first Sam's Wholesale Club opened in Oklahoma City in April 1983. The store name was later changed to Sam's Club. Walton was so excited about starting the new chain that he was like a child with a new toy. He loved the excitement and chaos of putting a new idea to work. It was another challenge for him, almost like building another company. By 1987, there were more than eighty Sam's Club stores.

Richest Man in America

The chances Walton took with the company contributed to its success. As a result, more people wanted to buy the company's stock, and the stock price increased. Because Walton and his family were the largest holders of the company's stock, this dramatically increased their wealth. In 1985, *Forbes* magazine named Walton, who was worth $2.8 billion, the richest man in America. Walton, however, did not like the title. He did not want attention drawn to him for his wealth. It was due mainly to the value of his stock, which he knew he would never sell. Besides, his ambition was to build the company rather than to acquire personal wealth.

He feared that if he began to concentrate on how much money he was personally making, it would take his focus off serving the customer, and it was his dedication to serving customers that had made the company successful. "We certainly have had more than adequate funds in this family for a long time—even before we got Wal-Mart cranked up," he said. "Here's the thing: money has never meant that much to me, not even in the sense of keeping score."[10] He defined being rich as having enough money for food, a nice house, and education for his children, as well as room for his dogs and a place to play tennis.

Walton's views were reflected in the lifestyle he led. He drove a pickup truck that had cages in the back for his hounds to ride in when he went hunting. He wore shoes that he got from Wal-Mart, and his favorite hat was a Wal-Mart baseball cap. He got his hair cut at a local barber shop, and his phone number was listed in the local telephone directory because he wanted to be available for associates to call with concerns or ideas.

Although Forbes *magazine named Walton the richest man in America in 1985, he still drove this pickup truck and wore shoes that he got from Wal-Mart.*

Walton was philosophical when the stock market crashed in October 1987 and his fortune plummeted by half a billion dollars. Since the drop in his fortune was due to the drop in the value of Wal-Mart stock, which he would never sell, he did not worry about it.

On the job, Walton did not expect to be treated better than other store executives. He did not ask for special treatment because he did not want other employees to resent him. When he was named the richest man in America, he worried that the title would affect his relationship with the people who worked in his stores. Instead of being jealous of him, however, they rallied around him. They were proud that he had achieved this milestone.

Sam Walton had a humble, folksy personality, but he was a sharp businessman who was worth $2.8 billion in 1985.

Walton's simple lifestyle sometimes made him seem unsophisticated. He was, however, an extremely sharp businessman who constantly assessed everything he saw. Underneath his folksy exterior Walton knew what he wanted to do and how to get it done.

Criticism

Not everyone was excited about Walton's success and the number of Wal-Mart and Sam's Club stores that were opened across the nation. Walton was frequently criticized for the number of home-town businesses that closed after a Wal-Mart came to town. There were fears that Wal-Mart was destroying the character—and economy—of small-town America.

Walton's view was that he helped small-town economies because his stores provided jobs and saved people money. Walton also pointed out that Wal-Mart kept customers from having to drive to large cities to visit discount stores.

Walton believed the changing face of the retail business in small towns across America was not due to Wal-Mart. It was due to the fact that customers wanted to get the best deal. If Wal-Mart had not found a way to give customers low prices, he noted, someone else would have. Small-town businesses could not look the same and do things the same way year after year, just as businesses in big cities could not. Walton himself had once been a store owner in a small town, and had seen that the future of retail was in discount stores. Instead of fighting it, he had embraced it.

Walton's critics said Wal-Marts destroyed the character and economy of small-town America by forcing hometown businesses that could not compete with the discount store to close.

Although labor unions have challenged Wal-Mart on several business practices, the company's employees have never formed a union.

Union Concerns

Another criticism of Wal-Mart came from labor unions. Labor unions wanted Wal-Mart truck drivers and other employees to become members, and also wanted Wal-Mart stores to be built by union members.

Walton did not want his workers to belong to unions because he felt unions would hurt communication between different levels of employees. He feared that unions would pit managers against other employees and keep them from sharing ideas about how to improve the company. He felt that he treated employees as partners by giving them the opportunity to buy Wal-Mart stock and share in the company's profits. He did not think unions needed to get involved. His employees usually agreed with him. When some Wal-Mart employees voted on whether or not to form a union, the unions were always voted down.

Female and Minority Workers at Wal-Mart

Another criticism of the way Walton ran his company had to do with the lack of women or members of minority groups in top management positions in the company. In the mid-1980s, there were no women or members of minority groups on its board of directors. Walton preferred to have the top executives in his company be people he was close to. His board of directors included his brother and son, as well as bankers he had worked with for a long time. It also included other men who had retail backgrounds.

Walton made Hillary Clinton Wal-Mart's first female board member in 1986 in response to shareholder complaints that there were no women on the company's board of directors.

The makeup of the board of directors did not sit well with shareholders. At one annual meeting in the mid-1980s, the crowd cheered when it was suggested that a woman be placed on the company's board of directors. Walton responded by making Hillary Clinton Wal-Mart's first female board member in 1986. Clinton tried to convince the company to promote more women to top positions. She had some success, and two women were named to vice president positions in the late 1980s.

Buy America

Walton was also criticized for having too many products in his stores that were made in foreign countries. In response to that criticism, and because he knew that many products overseas were made in factories with awful working conditions, he started a Buy America program. He made a commitment to buying as many products as possible from companies that made their goods in the United States. When a shirt maker in Arkansas was about to close because of competition from a factory in China, Walton placed a large order. The company was able to add employees instead of closing down. Walton claimed that his Buy America program created or preserved thousands of jobs.

Buy America was a business move as well. If people were employed, they had more money to shop at Wal-Mart. The program also encouraged American companies to lower their prices in order to compete with factories overseas. In turn, the overseas manufacturers lowered their prices even further. Wal-Mart benefited by buying goods even more cheaply.

Charitable Giving

The Buy America program helped improve Wal-Mart's image. Walton did not want the company to be thought of as a heartless corporation—he wanted it to seem just as friendly as a neighborhood variety store. In another attempt to accomplish this, he established the Wal-Mart Foundation in 1981, at the urging of Helen Walton. In 1987, the foundation gave more than $4 million to charity. Wal-Mart sponsored educational scholarships for the children of its employees and for high school seniors in communities where Wal-Mart stores were located.

Many of these gifts were given anonymously, or with the request that no publicity accompany the donation because

Criticized for having too many of his stores' products made in foreign countries, Walton responded by promising to buy as many American-made products as possible.

David Glass (pictured) became the chief executive officer of Wal-Mart in 1988 when, at the age of seventy, Walton decided to step down.

The Wal-Mart Foundation has provided millions of dollars in scholarships and Sam and Helen Walton have made personal contributions to a variety of arts, environmental, and veterans' organizations.

Walton did not want his company to be thought of as a place where anyone could go for an easy handout. He and his wife made donations to educational institutions, symphonies, environmental groups, and veterans' organizations, as well as art and theater groups. He also founded a special scholarship program for more than one hundred students from Central America to attend college in Arkansas. At their own expense, the Waltons built an exercise facility for Wal-Mart employees in Bentonville.

Slowing Down

After decades at the helm of Wal-Mart, Walton finally began to slow down. In 1988, at the age of seventy, he made David Glass the company's chief executive officer. Walton, however, continued to reach out to employees and try to make them enthusiastic about the company. He thrived on Saturday morning meetings and flying over cities to scout out the best locations for new Wal-Marts. He also loved to go over sales figures, find trouble spots, and come up with solutions. As he had his entire life, no matter where he was, he would stop in a store and check out the competition. When he went on an Alaskan cruise with his family, he was restless because he did not have any stores to check out.

By 1990, Walton had 1,528 stores, and Wal-Mart was doing $26 billion in annual sales. Even with this company that never seemed to stop growing, Walton had a knack for keeping the important small-company ideas alive. He had the same focus he had as a small-town merchant: making the customer happy.

51

Cancer Diagnosis

Walton had a little more free time now that he had handed some of his leadership duties over to Glass, and he spent some of it hunting and playing tennis. In the late 1980s, he began to feel aches in his bones. After he felt especially sore following a hunting trip, he went to the doctor. In early 1990, he found that he had an incurable type of bone cancer. Walton was treated with chemotherapy and radiation, but the treatments could only slow, not cure, the disease. As the cancer progressed, he became weaker, and moving became more painful.

Although Walton knew the disease would be fatal, he did not dwell on that. He was determined to make the most of the time he had left. He knew that his family would be well cared for after he died, thanks to the shares of Wal-Mart stock they owned. He wanted to make sure that everything was in order at Wal-Mart to give it the best chance for success after he was gone.

Putting Things in Order

Walton did everything he could to accomplish this goal. He estimated how much money Wal-Mart would be making years after his death. He also recorded his thoughts about running a business in an autobiography. He had set aside the project in the past, but now felt it was important to pass on his ideas.

Faced with death, Walton sometimes wondered if he had lived his life the right way. He questioned whether all the time he had devoted to Wal-Mart had been worth it. He decided it had. He felt that his commitment to free enterprise and low prices had improved people's quality of life. "I am just awfully proud of the whole deal and I feel good about how I chose to expend my energies in life,"[11] he said.

Walton had begun his retail career as a hands-on business owner and ended it that way. He looked forward to making some aspect of the business better each day. He never stopped setting goals. He decided if he were faced with the same choices again, he would make the same decisions.

Walton grew weaker as the disease progressed. When he accepted the medal of freedom from President George Bush at a ceremony in 1992, it was difficult for him to stand. A few days later he entered the University of Arkansas hospital in Little Rock. His interest in his company remained with him until the end. One

President George Bush presented Walton (left), who was weakened from treatments for bone cancer, with the Medal of Freedom in 1992. Just days later, the businessman died.

The pep rallies Walton organized to motivate Wal-Mart associates are just one of several business practices that have been adopted by many American companies.

of his last visitors was a local Wal-Mart manager, and Walton discussed sales figures with him.

Walton died on April 5, 1992, at the age of seventy-four. He had taken Wal-Mart to the top of the retail business. He had fulfilled the American dream of becoming successful through hard work, smart decisions, and a bit of luck. He left a fortune worth $2.5 billion and a company that changed the American retail scene.

Walton's Legacy

Many retailers tried to copy Walton's business practices and success. His enthusiasm made corporate pep rallies part of doing business in many American companies. His success in bringing in customers by offering the lowest price on goods led others to open giant bookstores, electronics stores, and music stores that also promised low prices.

Walton's insistence on giving customers the lowest possible price put power in the hands of consumers. Because Wal-Mart had so many stores and bought so much merchandise, it was able to use its clout to get companies to lower their prices. These savings were passed on to customers. It also helped customers get the products they wanted. For example, when a Wal-Mart associate learned that Hispanic customers wanted a cookware item called a *caldero*, it was put into stores.

Walton's son Rob became chairman of Wal-Mart upon his father's death. The company was run by David Glass, its president and chief executive officer. Glass retired as chief executive officer in 2000, and Lee Scott took over the company's top post.

Most Admired Company

The company became even more powerful after Walton's death. So many merchandise suppliers want to visit Wal-Mart headquarters that there are two daily nonstop flights from New York to Bentonville. By contrast, there are no daily nonstop flights to Little Rock, the state capital of Arkansas.

In 2003, *Fortune* magazine named Wal-Mart the most admired company in America. The businesspeople polled by the magazine were impressed by Wal-Mart's dynamic growth and ability to adhere to the same principles Walton founded it under. The company was five times the size it had been when Walton died in 1992, but remained focused on low prices and keeping its costs down.

Wal-Mart was doing $240 billion in annual sales and employed 1.3 million associates. In twenty-one states, Wal-Mart employed more people than any other company. It sold the most DVDs, groceries, diamonds, toys, video games, and toothpaste of any company in the nation. It also developed the most film and served the most people with optical services.

The company retained the cost-saving attitude that Walton had insisted upon. There were few frills for employees at the company's Bentonville headquarters. People who bought goods for the

Above: Sam Walton believed his commitment to free enterprise and low prices improved the quality of people's lives. Today, Wal-Mart serves millions of customers across America.

Opposite: Rob Walton became chairman of Wal-Mart after his father's death in 1992.

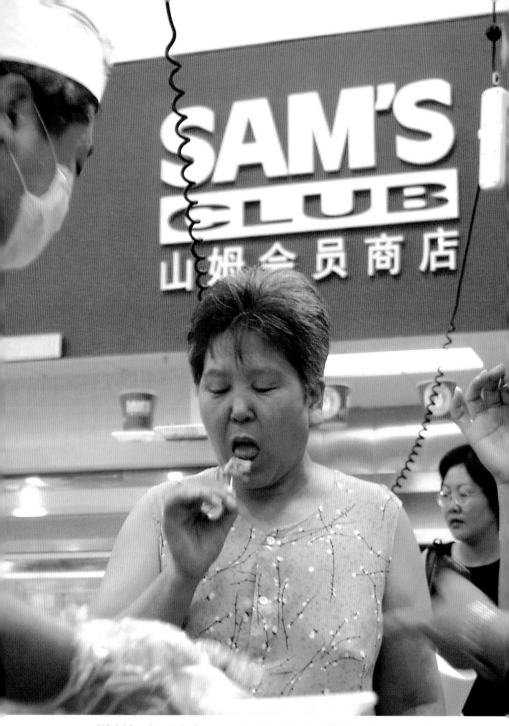

Wal-Mart's global expansion to Mexico, China, Japan, and Britain includes stores such as this Sam's Club in Beijing, China.

store met with suppliers in small cubicles. The suppliers were not treated to coffee or soda—they had to buy their own.

Walton's eagerness to try new ideas also lived on. Wal-Mart stores tried selling used cars, computers, and money orders. It experimented with flower delivery and Internet access.

Wal-Mart continued to be plagued by challenges from unions. Lawsuits charged that it underpaid employees and made them work unpaid overtime. There were also accusations that Wal-Mart did not pay female employees as well as it did male employees, and that women were not given as many opportunities for promotion. Wal-Mart executives pointed to the company's large workforce as evidence that it was a good place to work.

Poised for More Growth

As big as it was, Wal-Mart's chief executive officer felt the company could grow even more. "Could we be two times larger? Could we be three times larger?" Scott asked. "I think so."[12] It began opening Small-Marts, neighborhood markets that were much smaller than a typical Wal-Mart store. The company's idea was to open many of these smaller stores in a community, giving people a convenient place to shop for a few groceries or other items.

Scott also saw the potential for opening more Supercenters, which offered both groceries and general merchandise and were located mainly in the Southeast. Wal-Mart was also growing globally. In 2003, it was the leading retailer in Mexico. It also had stores in Japan, China, and Britain.

Walton's commitment to keeping prices low lives on at his stores and continues to bring in customers. His dedication to his company continues to be reflected in the hardworking Wal-Mart staff. His attitude toward company growth brought Wal-Mart to communities across the United States and beyond, which made shopping at Wal-Mart an everyday experience for millions of customers. Walton's influence stretches across America, and around the world.

IMPORTANT DATES

1918   Samuel Moore Walton is born on March 29 near
        Kingfisher, Oklahoma.

1936   Walton graduates from Hickman High School in
        Columbia, Missouri. He enters the University of Missouri
        in Columbia.

1940   After graduating with a degree in economics from the
        University of Missouri, Walton begins his career in retail
        as a management trainee at the J.C. Penney store in Des
        Moines, Iowa. He works at the store for eighteen months.

1942   Walton takes a job at a gunpowder factory near Tulsa,
        Oklahoma. He meets Helen Robson, his future wife.

1942   Walton begins his service in the U.S. Army during
        World War II.

1943   Walton and Helen Robson are married in Claremore,
        Oklahoma, on February 14.

1944   Samuel Robson Walton, the couple's first child, is born.

1945   Walton leaves the military and buys a Ben Franklin
        business in Newport, Arkansas.

1946   John Thomas Walton is born.

1948   James Carr Walton is born.

1949   Alice Walton is born.

1950   Walton is unable to renew the lease on his Ben Franklin
        store building. Walton buys a store in Bentonville,
        Arkansas, and calls it Walton's Five and Dime.

1952   Another Walton's Five and Dime is opened in Fayetteville,
        Arkansas. It is a self-service store.

1954   With his brother Bud, Walton opens a variety store in a
        shopping center in Ruskin Heights, Missouri.

IMPORTANT DATES

1962   Wal-Mart Discount City opens in Rogers, Arkansas.

1970   Wal-Mart stock is offered for sale.

1974   Walton gives retirement a try. He appoints Ronald M. Mayer as the leader of Wal-Mart Stores.

1976   Walton returns to his leadership role at Wal-Mart Stores.

1977   Walton closes his last variety store.

1979   Wal-Mart reaches the $1 billion mark in sales.

1983   The first Sam's Wholesale Club opens in Oklahoma City.

1985   *Forbes* names Walton the richest man in America. His fortune is estimated at $2.8 billion.

1988   David Glass is named chief executive officer of Wal-Mart Stores. Walton remains chairman of the board.

1990   Walton is diagnosed with a form of bone cancer.

1992   President George Bush honors Walton with the Medal of Freedom. Walton dies a few days later, on April 5, at the age of seventy-four.

FOR MORE INFORMATION

BOOKS

H.W. Brands, *Masters of Enterprise: Giants of American Business from John Jacob Astor and J.P. Morgan to Bill Gates and Oprah Winfrey.* New York: Free Press, 1999.

Bob Ortega, *In Sam We Trust.* New York: Random House, 1998.

Robert Slater, *The Wal-Mart Decade.* New York: Penguin, 2003.

Sam Walton with John Huey, *Sam Walton: Made in America: My Story.* New York: Doubleday, 1992.

PERIODICALS

Nicholas Stein, "America's Most Admired Companies: All Hail Starbucks, P&G, Dell—and of Course, New No. 1 Wal-Mart," *Fortune*, March 3, 2003.

Jerry Useem, "One Nation Under Wal-Mart," *Fortune*, March 3, 2003.

VIDEOS

"Sam Walton: Bargain Billionaire," A&E, *Biography*, Dec. 2, 1997.

NOTES

1. Sam Walton with John Huey, *Sam Walton: Made in America: My Story*, New York: Doubleday, 1992, p. 5.

2. Walton with Huey, *Sam Walton: Made in America*, p. 15.

3. Walton with Huey, *Sam Walton: Made in America*, p. 19.

4. Walton with Huey, *Sam Walton: Made in America*, p. 38.

5. Walton with Huey, *Sam Walton: Made in America*, p. 115.

6. Walton with Huey, *Sam Walton: Made in America*, p. 196.

7. Walton with Huey, *Sam Walton: Made in America*, p. 157.

8. Walton with Huey, *Sam Walton: Made in America*, p. 158.

9. Vance H. Trimble, *Sam Walton: The Inside Story of America's Richest Man,* New York: Dutton, 1990, p. 211.

10. Walton with Huey, *Sam Walton: Made in America*, p. 7.

11. Walton with Huey, *Sam Walton: Made in America*, p. 253.

12. Jerry Useem, "One Nation Under Wal-Mart," *Fortune,* March 3, 2003, p. 64.

INDEX